Do We Need the IMF and the World Bank?

SIR ALAN WALTERS

IEA
Institute of Economic Affairs
1994

First published in September 1994
by
THE INSTITUTE OF ECONOMIC AFFAIRS
2 Lord North Street, Westminster, London SW1P 3LB

© The Institute of Economic Affairs 1994

Current Controversies No. 10

All rights reserved

ISBN 0-255 36339-7

Printed in Great Britain by
GORON PRO-PRINT CO LTD, LANCING, WEST SUSSEX
Set in Bembo 11 on 13 point

Contents

FOREWORD .... *Colin Robinson* 4
THE AUTHOR 6
1. Bretton Woods Redux 7
2. Reputations 8
3. The Rôles of the Fund and the Bank 9
4. The IMF as an Insurance Fund 10
5. McNamara's Bank and Conditionality 12
   Pressure on Loan Targets 14
6. Politics and Integrity 15
   Romania: 'Resurrection of the Dead' 16
7. Bank Reform 18
   A Portfolio Cap? 20
8. IMF Reform 20
9. A Final Word 22
SUMMARY .... *Back Cover*

Foreword

Two powerful international institutions – the International Monetary Fund (IMF) and the World Bank – have considerable influence over the economic fortunes of many countries. The IMF provides short-term 'balance-of-payments' assistance, and the Bank gives longer-term development loans. Creditor countries have found it convenient to channel assistance through the Fund and the Bank to avoid accusations that they were bullying poor countries into accepting onerous conditions on their loans.

In *Current Controversies* No.10, Sir Alan Walters – best known in Britain as former adviser to Mrs (now Lady) Thatcher but also former economic adviser to the World Bank and one of the most distinguished of British economists – considers the performance of these two international institutions on their fiftieth anniversaries.

He points our that attempts to downsize them '...always end up making them bigger' (p.8) even though the rationale for the IMF, in particular, virtually disappeared when currencies were floated in September 1971. Despite the professional competence and integrity of their staff, Sir Alan is sceptical not only of the proposal that they should undertake new functions but of whether they should continue with the functions they now perform.

There is no shortage of suggestions for new tasks. In July 1994, in one of those periodic outbreaks of the desire to 'manage' exchange rates, a Bretton Woods Commission report hankered after a régime in which the IMF would monitor and control exchange rate movements. Sir Alan describes that proposal as 'unwise' since he sees no way the Fund's 'philosopher kings' could avoid the supposed 'excesses' of the market (p.8).

Sir Alan sees dangers in assistance given by both the Fund and the Bank at subsidised interest rates. The Fund does not penalise recidivists: the Bank's conditions are often mere window-dressing because the interests of its officials and those of the recipient countries ensure that true 'conditionality' is rarely invoked. Politicisation is a general danger, particularly noticeable recently in the case of Russia where normal loan conditions have been significantly relaxed.

There is a case for abolishing both Fund and Bank. Indeed, in Sir Alan's view they are relics of the time before people had realised the advantages of '...getting government and politics out of monetary policy and finance' (p.22). It would be a 'tall order indeed' to ask them to carry '...the immense burden of managing the world's currencies and exchange rates' (p.22).

But, since he sees no immediate prospect of abolition, he suggests some practical proposals for reform, such as capping the portfolios of both institutions to restrict new lending; shifting growth in new loans to the International Finance Corporation (which makes loans without government guarantee to the private sector); turning the IMF into a 'genuine insurance institution' (p.21) which charges near-market rates for countries which persistently reschedule, or into an institution which gives credit ratings but does not provide subsidised loans.

The *Current Controversies* series is designed to encourage discussion of topical and important issues. There is no doubt that Sir Alan's concise and stimulating paper about the IMF and Bank – written from the viewpoint of someone who knows the institutions from the inside – will fulfil that function. The views expressed are, of course, those of the author, not of the IEA (which has no corporate view), its Trustees, Directors or Advisers.

September 1994   COLIN ROBINSON
Editorial Director, Institute of Economic Affairs;
Professor of Economics, University of Surrey

The Author

SIR ALAN WALTERS has been Vice Chairman and Director of AIG Trading Group, Inc., since 1991. He was Chief Economic Adviser to the Prime Minister (on secondment), 1981-84 and 1989. He was appointed as a Lecturer in Econometrics at the University of Birmingham in 1952, and Professor of Econometrics and Head of the Department of Econometrics and Social Statistics in 1961. Subsequently he was Sir Ernest Cassel Professor of Economics in the University of London (at the LSE), 1968-76, and Professor of Economics at the Johns Hopkins University, Baltimore, Maryland, 1976-91. Since 1984, he has been a Senior Fellow at the American Enterprise Institute.

Among his numerous appointments, he has been a Consultant to the Governments of Israel, Singapore and Malaysia, and to the Economic Commission for Asia and the Far East. He has held various visiting professorships and was Economic Adviser to the World Bank, 1976-80, 1984-88.

He has contributed widely to professional and learned journals, and his books (as author, contributor or editor) include: *Growth without Development* (1966); *An Introduction to Econometrics* (1969, 2nd edn. 1971); *Noise and Prices* (1974); *Microeconomic Theory* (1977); and *Britain's Economic Renaissance* (1986).

He is an Honorary Fellow of the Institute of Economic Affairs, which has published his *Integration in Freight Transport* (1968), *Money in Boom and Slump* (1969, 3rd edn. 1971), *Economists and the British Economy* (1978), 'Land Speculator – Creator or Creature of Inflation?', in *Government and the Land* (1974), 'In Thrall to Creditors?', in *Crisis '75...?* (1975). In 1990, the IEA and Fontana published his *Sterling in Danger*.

Currently he writes a monthly newsletter, *AIG Trading Corp. Market Advisory* (AIG, Greenwich, Connecticut); and he contributes a regular column to the IEA's journal, *Economic Affairs*.

Do We Need the IMF and the World Bank?
SIR ALAN WALTERS

Bretton Woods Redux

AT THE END OF the World Bank-IMF meetings in October 1993, there was a meeting of the so-called Bretton Woods Commission. Chaired by Paul Volcker, it was a gathering of former central bankers and finance ministers and various distinguished economists known to yearn for some system of controlled exchange rates. In view of history (from the last three months to the last 30 years), this is surprising. But notwithstanding the lessons of history, this Committee represents an influential body of opinion. The general view is that exchange rates should not be left to the market but should be guided by governments in 'target zones' which correspond to the valuation put on currencies by suitable monitoring agencies.[1] The Bretton Woods Commission (BWC) reported in July 1994.[2]

The BWC report duly concluded that the monetary authorities for the three main currencies (dollar, Deutschemark and yen) should 'establish a more formal system of coordination involving firm and credible commitments to support these policy improvements and avoid excessive exchange rate misalignments and volatility'. And 'In time this system could possibly involve flexible exchange rate bands within which exchange rates could move without mandating a policy response'.

The obvious international institution to monitor world currencies is, as the BWC asserted, the International Monetary

---

[1] For a whole coterie of distinguished authors, see 'Rethinking Bretton Woods: A New World System', *International Economic Insights*, Washington: The Institute for International Economics, September/October 1993.

[2] Bretton Woods Commission, *Bretton Woods: Looking to the Future, Commission Report*, Washington DC, 1994.

Fund (IMF) aided perhaps by its complementary institution, the World Bank (the Bank). Indeed not merely the monitoring but also the *management* of currencies, through its agents the governments, would be the ideal rôle of the IMF and the Bank. Then all currencies could be kept within the bounds calculated by the economists of the IMF as the tolerable limits of 'fundamental real equilibrium exchange rates'. Thus would market 'excesses' be avoided by the Fund's philosopher kings.

However unwise the structure of such an international monetary system, it would be rash to dismiss it as impossible. At the very least we should cast a sceptical eye over these institutions to see how they perform. That is the purpose of this paper.

Reputations

UNLIKE OLD SOLDIERS, international institutions never fade away, they grow ever larger and ever more powerful. Nowhere is this tendency more obvious than in the great institutions of the United Nations and the two creations of Bretton Woods, the Bank and the IMF. All attempts to downsize them end up by making them bigger.

World governments and the financial community have not been seen persistently to oppose the development and growth of the Bretton Woods institutions. In part, this is because of the professional competence and integrity of the staff – a startling contrast with such politicised offshoots of the United Nations as UNESCO, WHO, FAO, UNCTAD. No doubt, also, there is the usual jobs-for-the-boys reason. But above all, is the belief that the Fund and Bank as supposedly amorphous international institutions can be used to induce debtor countries to adopt policies (and in particular 'structural adjustments') which creditor nations individually, or even as a group, perhaps could not themselves impose. In the delicate diplomacy of ex-colonies turned independent states, it is not considered good form for large Western creditor nations to 'bully' struggling Third World states. But the Bank and Fund, in which virtually all countries have an interest, and their own staff, are largely acceptable alternative taskmasters.

Of course, many debtor countries, particularly socialist states, have been annoyed by the conditionality and, on occasion, the arrogance of these institutions. But I think it is clear they would have been much more annoyed with face-to-face confrontation with their creditor's (gunboat!) statement of the conditions. Grumbles about the Bank and the Fund being merely agents of the G7 still appear. But, as with the efforts to downsize them, so attempts to demonise these institutions have been unsuccessful.

The Rôles of the Fund and the Bank

THE FUND IS NOT A FUND, of course: it is a bank. And the Bank is not a bank: it is a fund. Originally in 1944, the IMF was designed to provide short-term assistance to countries whose currencies were pegged to gold or the US dollar. Countries which, through no fault of their own, found themselves running short of foreign exchange (dollars) could get limited short-term assistance from the Fund by drawing down their balances and by swaps. In turn, the borrowing country would undertake to pursue policies that were expected to restore its reserves and confidence – the 'conditionality'. Exchange rates were not intended to be fixed in tablets of stone. The fathers of Bretton Woods anticipated there would be changes in rates in response to a 'fundamental disequilibrium', but in fact countries were generally reluctant to move their dollar/gold parities. What was intended as a pegged but adjustable rate of exchange usually became rigid and fixed – with all the ensuing troubles that were implied.

The Bank, *per contra*, was established to provide long-term capital flows to help the reconstruction of war-devastated countries: its official name, the International Bank for Reconstruction and Development, spelt out the intentions of the founders. It soon found its rôle as a lender to devastated Europe taken over. Its loans were, of course, dwarfed first by official flows, in the form of Marshall Aid, and later by the gradual development from the 1960s onwards of private capital movements. But lending to Third World countries became the core of its operations from the 1950s.

Although the rationale for the IMF disappeared when virtually all the world's currencies were floated after the United States went off gold in September 1971, this had little or no effect on the Fund. Although there was no pegged parity to defend, countries still had an appetite for short-term borrowing to buttress reserves eroded by their profligacy or bad luck. 'Managed' exchange rates or dirty floats were the order of the days of the 1970s. The IMF was seen as a sort of insurance arrangement to enable countries to survive the trials and tribulations of rapidly changing markets without having dramatic changes, unwanted by governments, in monetary policy (interest rates) or the exchange rate. Of course, the IMF had no effect on the really important exchange rate changes which are widely (although incorrectly) alleged to have caused such tumult, namely the dollar/mark and dollar/yen. These creditor countries toed no IMF line. The Fund was still in the business of disciplining debtors rather than creditors.

Perhaps the Fund's finest hour was in the Third World debt crisis that erupted after Mexico defaulted on her interest payments in August 1982. The creditor countries, principally the United States, found the IMF a most useful intermediary; the Fund could specify conditionality that, if laid down by the United States, would have been unacceptable as 'Yankee neo-imperialism'. Equally the debtor countries saw that their interests had a suitable voice through the Fund and the Bank representatives.

The IMF as an Insurance Fund

AS REMARKED ABOVE, THE FUND was set up originally to induce some international discipline in exchange rates. The main fear in 1944 was that there would be competitive devaluations, multiple rates and all the other discriminatory and self-defeating currency, capital and trade restrictions characteristic of the years between the two world wars. The Fund was to act as an insurance arrangement: countries which, through no fault of their own, were in payment difficulties would be able to draw on the Fund to tide them over. Thus they could avoid unwarranted devaluations and trade restrictions.

By its very nature, IMF assistance was given at a subsidised interest rate, in the sense that the rate charged was below that which the country could obtain on the international capital markets. The subsidies have both widened and deepened over time. The original lending under the Standby or Extended Arrangements was for one to three years and subject to phasing and conditionality. But, particularly for poor countries, the strings have been much loosened, for example in the Structural Adjustment Facility (SAF) established in March 1986 and the Enhanced Structural Adjustment Facility (ESA) of 1988. The former extends credit to the rulers of poor countries for 10 years at a rate of 0·5 per cent, with very weakened conditionality. The general trend since the mid-1970s has been more subsidies and looser conditions.

This presents a dilemma. Countries that are in difficulties through no fault of their own – by accident, so to speak – will enjoy a subsidy, but clearly in a sense they deserve one. The real difficulty occurs when countries pursue policies that are politically attractive to the ruling élite, but which inevitably get them into difficulties with payments and debt servicing. Then it is the government's fault, but such profligacy is the road to subsidised credit.

The Fund has to be ostensibly non-discriminatory in providing assistance and, unlike the traditional central bank, cannot supply funds at penal rates. So, in order to ration access, the Fund uses 'conditionality', as explained earlier. Many international commentators and IMF staff believe that fierce conditionality adequately discourages Third World governments from pursuing policies that are beyond their means and which impoverish their populace. A distinguished staff member of the Fund told me that a visit to a debtor country that was going through the agony of rescheduling was enough to convince anyone that such a desperate state would not be lightly courted.

This view, however, depends on the supposition that the rulers of a Third World country are primarily concerned with the welfare of their subjects. This may well apply to those few countries where democratic or other representative institutions provide *some* check on the government pursuing policies of mass immiseration. But the majority of Third World countries have no semblance of democracy. Their rulers are free to pursue policies which feather their own nests at the expense of the people. We are all familiar with Presidents Marcos, Mobutu, Nkruma, Samoza, *et al.* It was financially useful to get an IMF loan, just as it was politically convenient to blame the IMF for the stringent measures of austerity that ensued.

But the important question was: Did the rulers learn from the experience of defaulting and *mend their ways*? Was the IMF instrumental in inducing reforms which would otherwise not have occurred? Because of ambient economic events, such as changes in terms of trade, and political developments, it is impossible to give a persuasive answer. But what we *do* know is that there is a considerable concentration of IMF assistance on a few countries. Some eight years ago, Roland Vaubel of the University of Mannheim showed[3] that from 1960 to 1982, 42 member countries (out of a total of around 150) accounted for 78 per cent of all standby and extended credits. And the staff of the IMF showed that 24 countries received credits for more than 10 *consecutive* years.

Countries that get into difficulties tend to be recidivists. After a few years they again experience payments problems and again have to reschedule with IMF assistance. This is no accident or random event. These 20 per cent of countries that were recedivists – always in severe financial straits – were demonstrably 'bad risks' and in any normal market they would be required to pay much more for the insurance cover of the IMF. But the IMF is very limited in the extent to which it can discriminate between high- and low-risk nations, so the Fund has 'adverse selection' of the perennial paupers – the subjects, of course, not the rulers.

McNamara's Bank and Conditionality

LIKE THE IMF, World Bank and International Development Association (IDA) loans are subsidised. The Bank can afford to

---

[3] R. Vaubel, 'The Political Economy of the International Monetary Fund', in R. Vaubel and T.D. Willett (eds.), *The Political Economy of International Organizations: A Public Choice Approach*, Boulder, Col.: Westview Press, 1991, pp.204-44.

subsidise since its capital is given *gratis*; no dividends are paid to the shareholding countries. On the basis of the guarantees, the Bank can raise money as an AAA rated institution at very low cost. In principle, the Bank lends the foreign exchange component of a project – although this principle has been eroded over the years. The domestic counterpart resources are required to be financed by the borrowing government. With structural adjustment lending the objective is usually balance-of-payments support, but this is often simply another way of filling gaping holes in the government's budget. The Bank supervises projects to ensure that the money is spent in accordance with the project and requires authority for any substantial expenditure over budget.[4]

Unlike the IMF, the Bank generally saddles its loans with all sorts and varieties of conditions which are concerned with development in the broadest possible sense. The usual conditionality for a public utility investment is that the prices somehow cover the costs, that they follow good accounting practices, that there is a systematic maintenance programme, and so on. But conditionality has been the stuff of fads and fashions. For example, in the last few years of Robert McNamara (President of the Bank from 1968 to 1980), virtually all project loans had to have a population-control component. And for many years a project has had to prove that it alleviates poverty – at least ostensibly – by various directed benefits and redistributional policies. Birth control was *de rigeur* for many projects, however absurd that might be. All these curious conditionalities reflected the shifting fashions of the patrons.

But, generally, such conditionality was merely window-dressing. There were very few cases where conditionality was invoked, for example, to stop a second or third tranche of a loan. The Bank rarely pulled the plug – at least against the wishes of the borrowing government. This was partly a consequence of the way in which the loan programme was defined and managed, and partly a result of the incentives both in the Bank and in the recipient countries.

---

[4] In 1993, however, it was revealed that the Bank's new building in Washington DC was over-running the budget by more than 80 per cent. This did not enhance the Bank's reputation for project supervision.

Pressure on Loan Targets

The loan programme was determined largely by the President of the Bank. He decided how much money was to go to each country. These sums were translated into loan targets for country officers. And it was the job of the Bank staff to ensure that these loans were made – with all the trappings of poverty alleviation, birth control and other fads of the day.

It is not surprising a certain cynicism entered into the construction of conditionality. The pressure was on the loan officer and regional department to make sure they used up their quota of funds; on such a performance depended their budgets, status and staffing and (above all) their promotion. Making loans was the measure of performance in the Bank hierarchy; it came down from the President himself. On the other hand, the recipient country usually had treasury officials skilled in Bank procedures and criteria. Often they were either ex Bank staff or had spent a considerable time as attached staff at the Bank. They knew what was necessary to secure the subsidised loan. And they were judged by the amount of money they got from the Bank, usually in terms of commitments rather than disbursements.

Thus the loan officer and the treasury (or central bank) official could agree on conditionality which would satisfy the posturing of the patrons, knowing full well that it was unlikely to be implemented. Again there might be considerable window dressing; since the treasury officials normally control the information and statistics, this is a tempting solution which both sides at the operational level can implicitly agree. But even if the conditionality was being blatantly ignored, one could be reasonably sure that it would not be invoked to stop future disbursements or other potential loans. The pressure to meet the quotas would generally over-ride any qualms about 'quality'.

It is noteworthy that the new Bank management was clearly concerned about the quality of its loans and suspected that quantity had clear priority over quality. This was confirmed by an internal committee of senior rank, the Wapenhans committee, which reported last year that such concerns were by no means groundless.

But how to reform the system? The Wapenhans Report suggested that, in promoting staff, more attention should be paid to the quality as distinct from the quantity of loans, and many other 'good things'. I remain sceptical. With a bureaucracy as large as the Bank's, change is unlikely. Periodic 'reorganisations' at the Bank seem to have achieved little...and there is often a return with only cosmetic changes to the *status quo*.

The point is that Mr McNamara did know what he was doing when he structured the vastly expanding Bank on 'quantitative' as distinct from qualitative lines. He was used to this sort of management – body counts in Vietnam, condom counts in Calcutta, and so on – and he knew how a bureaucracy would respond. With such statistical controls, he could manipulate the vast bureaucracy. He was also aware that this was the best structure to press the Bank's case for an ever larger mandate, burgeoning staff and greater power – for the President in particular. It is difficult to see how the control and motivation of staff can be managed and directed through 'qualitative' judgements, and the trade-offs between quantity and quality (*ex post* and *ex ante*) controlled. So I suspect that, like the many other attempts to reform the Bank, this will also founder on the hard rock of bureaucratic obduracy.

But what about the shareholders? Nominally, reform of the Bank should be the ultimate responsibility of the shareholders – namely, the governments. Although the board occasionally asserted its power, McNamara dominated board decisions. That was not difficult to do. The board members were primarily interested in ensuring that Bank lending promoted their exports. A secondary, though not small, interest was in the Bank promoting their preferred nationals to lucrative and influential appointments in Washington...jobs for the boys. Provided they could adopt the protective clothing of the conditionality of poverty lending, the board was happy to agree to McNamara's policies that gave rise to more export promotion and more jobs in Washington.

Politics and Integrity

AS IS WELL KNOWN, the Fund and Bank are supposed to be above politics and certainly above party politics. Yet, as these institutions have grown in size, they have become increasingly tempting as political vehicles and targets. The suspicion that the IMF is largely dominated by the US banks has been voiced – and not only by Third World countries. The IMF has replaced the gunboat.

More substantial, however, is the accusation that the IMF serves as an agency which organises both commercial banks and creditor governments into one bargaining monopoly which confronts the debtor country. The debtor country finds it impossible to default on some loans while settling others. Many countries would find it advantageous to deal with the individual government, or if the debt is to a private corporation, with the individual lender as was the case in the 19th and early 20th centuries. But that is ruled out. It is an all-or-nothing proposition.

Perhaps the most obvious present case of politicisation of the Bank and Fund is in the loans for Russia. In their anxiety to bend to political pressure and lend to the former Soviet Union, the IMF and Bank have greatly relaxed their normal conditions. As *The Economist* has argued, there is no economic case for aid to Russia. The main reason for aid is to 'support Yeltsin' as what the Western governments perceive to be the best hope for Russian reform (just as they had hitherto embraced Yeltsin's arch-rival, Gorbachev, as the great Russian saviour).

Of course, politics cannot help intruding in the policies of the Bank and Fund. But what is wrong is to allow such politics to compromise the intellectual integrity of the institutions. Obviously, it is tempting to instruct staff that a favourable economic review of this or that country is required because of political considerations. But it is corrosive of professionalism and saps the institution's integrity.

Romania: 'Resurrection of the Dead'

Consider the following example. In 1978-79 the Bank sent a large mission to Romania to produce its 'first basic economic report' since it joined the Bank in 1972. The publication, *Romania: The Industrialization of an Agrarian Economy under Socialist Planning*, in 1979 claimed:

'Between 1950 and 1975 the economy grew rapidly within the framework of comprehensive economic planning, which was made possible by the state's control of the major productive resources ... through this control the state was able to mobilise the resources required ...'

'...between 1950 and 1975 the Romanian economy sustained one of the highest growth rates in the world...national income grew at 9·7 per cent per annum.'

'Between 1976 and 1980 national income is planned to grow at 10 to 11 per cent a year', and over 1981-90 'national income would grow at 8 to 8·4 per cent a year.'

This was obvious nonsense to any layman, let alone a trained economist. Indeed, it was pointed out that if one extrapolated back from the alleged *per capita* income of $1,170 in 1975 (itself a startling overestimate) at the 9·7 per cent rate, the income in 1950 was insufficient to support life. This was not economics: it was religion: it was the resurrection of the dead.

Many of the Bank staff involved knew that these claims were inconsistent with simple observation of the poverty of Romania. Travellers' tales were more informative than the 700-page Bank report. Mr McNamara was apprised of these assessments, yet he insisted on publication. The political motivations for such insistence we do not know; but the corruption of the institution's integrity was clear. Nor is the Romanian case an aberration; in the same year (1979) a similarly glowing report of the growth and prospects of Yugoslavia was published by the Bank.

In the 14 years since Robert McNamara left the Bank there have been three presidents, none of whom has had the commanding presence he enjoyed. There have been many bureaucratic shuffles around the turf. But in essence the Bank remains Mr McNamara's creation. Various political biases in research have continued — for example, until recently, a very low *per capita* income was attributed to China in order that she might qualify for highly subsidised IDA funds. But it is necessary to add that, where there is no overriding political interest, the Bank has published good and intellectually honest (although costly) accounts of many aspects of development. Its contributions on health and education, for example, have been both brave and incisive – and, incidentally, much at odds with the tastes of ruling élites – reflecting the high quality of much of the staff.

And in the hierarchy of similar institutions, the World Bank clearly leads – although the sceptic might justifiably conclude that that is not saying very much. The abysmal performance of the highly politicised African Development Bank (AfDB) has been recently highlighted in the press. The scandals of the European Bank for Reconstruction and Development (EBRD) are even better known. And no one could argue that the highly politicised Asian Development Bank (ADB) and the Inter American Development Bank (IADB) come near to the standards of the World Bank. They seem to suffer from bureaucratic malaise even more than their big brother.

Bank Reform

A CASE CAN BE (indeed, has been) made for abolishing the Bank and Fund.[5] Although the probability of such drastic reform is zero, it is worth examining the pros and cons. First, one should note that the funds commanded by the Bank and Fund are small compared with gross national products and gross domestic investment and with private capital flows. Indeed, all 'official development assistance' accounted for only 1·4 per cent of GNP for the whole world. For low income countries it was 3 per cent of their GNP, for middle income countries 0·7 per cent of GNP, and for upper income economies (such as Brazil) 0·1 per cent.[6] The end of World Bank lending would not be the end of the world. But it might well be the end of some of the Bank's favourite régimes.

---

[5] The most consistent and effective critic of these institutions is Lord Bauer whose work, *The Development Frontier*, Cambridge, Mass.: Harvard University Press, 1971, is essential reading. See also R. Vaubel, 'A Public Choice Approach to International Organization', *Public Choice*, Vol.51, 1986, pp.39-58.

[6] Source: *World Development Report*, Washington DC: World Bank, 1993.

Loans, although the main business of the Bank, are by no means its only function. Many observers would argue that the Bank has developed a most valuable rôle as a source of independent advice. The Bank's staff of experts – although in recent years somewhat contaminated by the need to achieve national representation rather than by selection on pure merit – has been a source of valuable advice on projects and programmes. Although the pressure to fulfil loan quotas undoubtedly does bias the conclusions on occasion (the egregious case of Romania is a case in point), the information and analysis of projects and programmes usually emerges quite clearly from the reports of the competent staff.

A dedicated free-marketeer would surely suggest that function can be done more efficaciously by the private sector. Perhaps so. But there are wayward incentives in the rôle of the private consultant. The profits to be made by a consulting firm, particularly where large infrastructure investments are concerned, are primarily from the design, supervision and contracting operations. Any firm, unless expressly excluded from subsequent work, will have an incentive to find a project both feasible and with benefits that clearly outweigh the costs. It is said, with only slight exaggeration, that they 'never see a project which they did not like' and propose yet more of such 'good thing(s)'.

Granted the Bank's useful rôle as honest broker, performing this task does not require that the Bank carry a loan portfolio. Indeed, in the absence of any pressure to lend, the Bank's integrity in reviewing projects would be enhanced not diminished. There are close analogues of this rôle in the credit rating agencies such as Standard and Poor's and Moody's. These agencies investigate the credit risk of corporations, their financial and investment programmes, without any thought of extending credit. The Bank could serve a similar need without any credit implications.

However good the arguments for winding down the size of the Bank, it is of course quite fanciful to suppose that the Bank – including the industrialised countries which have effective control – will ever eschew its rôle as a main supplier of subsidised credit. One is therefore driven to search for feasible and *possible* reforms rather than rational but impossible proposals.

A Portfolio Cap?

One feasible reform is to place an overall limit on the Bank's portfolio. Its cumulative lending amounts to about $270 billion, with normal annual increments around $13 billion. Such a reform is much more radical than it seems. The Bank has been expanding its loans for many years, and, if a portfolio cap were imposed, this would have a drastic effect on its new loan operations. Indeed, it might be feasible only to introduce the capping gradually. The reduction of loan extensions would enable the Bank to concentrate more on the 'qualitative' aspects of its portfolio, with compliance procedures and with disbursements. The Bank's own Wapenhans Report emphasised that these were neglected in the anxiety to make more loan commitments.

More specifically, the reform might shift any growth in the loan portfolio to the Bank's affiliate, the International Finance Corporation (IFC). Unlike the Bank, which can make loans only with a government guarantee, the IFC is charged with making loans, without such guarantee, to the private sector, and can and has taken equity stakes in many enterprises in the Third World. The shift would be consonant with widespread privatisation and the belief that most wealth creation must come through private enterprise.

IMF Reform

IN DISCUSSING REFORM, I deal with the Fund as it exists today – not the sort of institution which, according to the BWC recommendation, would be saddled with the tasks of world co-ordination of monetary and macro-economic policies.

Much of what has been said about the Bank applies, *mutatis mutandis*, to the Fund. *First*, the drastic medicine: could not the Fund be abolished? Or, as a second less nasty potion, could it not be absorbed into its big brother, the Bank? The case for abolition is that its original function has long gone in this floating world. The provision of hard currency subsidised loans for countries that find themselves in circumstances, not of their own choosing, short of international credit has been its main business – together with the much vaunted conditionality. The main distinction between the Bank and the Fund was once the terms of the credit – short for the Fund, long for the Bank. But with the Bank's development of 'structural adjustment loans' and with the more or less continuous oversight of the Fund, the two functions have overlapped. And in spite of quite close co-ordination, there have been turf battles, different advice and some waste.

The *second* alternative – of absorbing the Fund into the Bank – flies in the face of the widespread feeling that the Bank is too large. It is highly bureaucratic and lacks the flexibility of response of, for example, the IFC. Thus this option also requires that the Bank be pruned to a manageable size.

A *third*, but not mutually exclusive, approach, is to try to restructure the Fund as a genuine insurance institution. In order to discourage recidivists, the Fund should restructure the price it charges for assistance. At present the rate of interest rises as the quota and lines are drawn down. They are the same for all countries, whatever past performance and however high the rate of interest at which they can borrow may be. It would be an additional encouragement to pursue fiscally appropriate policies if interest rates were raised to near market levels for those countries that persistently reschedule. The IMF should simulate the operation of a private risk pool. At present the Fund (and Bank) use a dichotomy – credit worthy and not credit worthy – as a basic determinant of their policy. But, of course, at *some* interest rate even the basket cases may well be worthwhile borrowers.

A *fourth* alternative would be for the Fund to perform all its monitoring and research operations but not to engage in loan operations. Now, if the IMF lends to a country, it is a signal for other sovereign governments and, in most cases, for the private sector to follow the IMF lead. In a real sense the IMF gives a credit rating – together with conditionality on how to maintain or improve that rating. That task could be performed (as suggested for the Bank) without making subsidised loans – or in principle by making only small nominal loans.

A Final Word

AS DISTINCT FROM PRACTICAL POLICY, the ideal solution would be to abolish the Fund and the Bank – wind them up and disperse their expertise to other activities. The Bank and the Fund were the progeny of a generation that regarded government management of banking and finance as being the only way forward. Yet in the intervening years, we have become increasingly aware of the advantages of getting government and politics out of monetary policy and finance. The widespread and rapid movement towards independent central banks or towards currency board arrangements is the most obvious example of this change. Such independent central banks sit uncomfortably with institutions like the IMF and Bank which are dominated by political pressures.

No doubt the independent central banks will want to have some form of central bankers' bank, rather like the Bank for International Settlements for the OECD countries, to carry through various functions. But the important point is that this central bankers' bank be ruled by the central banks themselves and not by the constituent governments. This would not guarantee a completely non-politicised institution but, under the central bankers' guidance, they would have an incentive jealously to guard their prerogatives internationally as well as they do on a national platform.

So much for ideal solutions. They are but pipe dreams. It would be foolish to delude oneself about the possibilities of real reform – as distinct from nominal reshuffling – in these great international institutions. The practical, in contrast to the ideal, reforms I have emphasised – capping Bank and Fund total portfolios and differential interest rates related to market rates – are quite modest, but still unlikely. No doubt in time we shall hear from the Bretton Woods Commission on their proposed reforms for the Bank and the Fund in order that they can carry the immense burden of managing the world's currencies and exchange rates. That would be a tall order indeed.

CURRENT
CONTROVERSIES

No.1 Gordon Pepper, *Restoring Credibility: Monetary Policy Now*, ISBN 0-255 36311-7, October 1992, £2.50.

No.2 Forrest Capie, *Trade Wars: A Repetition of the Inter-War Years?*, ISBN 0-255 36313-3, December 1992, £2.00.

No.3 Colin Robinson, *Making a Market in Energy*, ISBN 0-255 36314-1, December 1992, £2.95.

No.4 Geoffrey E Wood, Terence C Mills and Forrest Capie, *Central Bank Independence: What Is It and What Will It Do For Us?*, ISBN 0-255 36315-X, January 1993, £2.95.

No.5 Stephen Glaister and Tony Travers, *New Directions for British Railways? The Political Economy of Privatisation and Regulation*, ISBN 0-255 36321-4, June 1993, £4.95.

No.6 John T Addison and W Stanley Siebert, *Social Engineering in the European Community: The Social Charter, Maastricht and Beyond*, ISBN 0-255 36323-0, July 1993, £3.95.

No.7 David Sawers, *Should the Taxpayer Support the Arts?*, ISBN 0-255 36325-7, September 1993, £3.95.

No.8 John Chown, Geoffrey Wood and Massimo Beber, *The Road to Monetary Union Revisited*, ISBN 0-255 36332-X, April 1994, £3.50.

No.9 Edwin G. West, *Britain's Student Loan System in World Perspective: A Critique*, ISBN 0-255 36335-4, June 1994, £4.00

New Title from the IEA

Britain's Student Loan System in World Perspective: A Critique

EDWIN G. WEST

1. Demand for university places is expanding in most countries faster than the ability of government to finance such expansion.

2. In Britain, the Chancellor has announced that student grants will increasingly be replaced by repayable loans. Students may soon have to pay some of their tuition fees as well as maintenance costs.

3. Spending on education should ideally be financed as an equity investment. Repayments by student borrowers should be contingent on income.

4. The British student loan system, however, is not income-contingent but entails *fixed* monthly instalments.

5. Repayment arrangements are inefficient and are likely to lead to serious default problems. Instead of using the income-tax machinery, collection is entrusted to a quango.

6. Although apparently a loan system, it incorporates concealed subsidies because repayment does not begin until the April after courses finish and because the real interest rate is zero.

7. There are better systems in other countries, especially New Zealand where there is an income-contingent scheme under which repayment is administered by the tax authorities and students pay a positive real interest rate.

8. In the British loan system '... new and disguised forms of government subsidies or grants are quickly emerging and are taking the form of increasing costs associated with the present loan structure'. (p.38)

9. To minimise administration costs and reduce a potentially high default burden, the income-tax machinery should be used to collect repayments.

10. To avoid concealed subsidies, students should be charged a positive real interest rate and loans should accumulate during the period they are being educated. 'To suppose otherwise would be openly to ignore the long-standing belief of economists that the time preference of potential lenders is normally positive.' (p.40)

ISBN 0-255 36335-4

Current Controversies No.9

£4.50 inc. P&P

IEA

The Institute of Economic Affairs
2 Lord North Street, Westminster
London SW1P 3LB
Telephone: 071-799 3745